Simple Science Projects

PROJECTS WITH

COLOR
AND LIGHT

By
John Williams

Illustrated by
Malcolm S. Walker

Gareth Stevens Children's Books
MILWAUKEE

84816

For a free color catalog describing Gareth Stevens' list of high-quality books, call 1-800-341-3569 (USA) or 1-800-461-9120 (Canada).

Titles in the Simple Science Projects series:

Simple Science Projects with Air
Simple Science Projects with Color and Light
Simple Science Projects with Electricity
Simple Science Projects with Flight
Simple Science Projects with Machines
Simple Science Projects with Time
Simple Science Projects with Water
Simple Science Projects with Wheels

Library of Congress Cataloging-in-Publication Data

Williams, John.
    Projects with color and light / John Williams : illustrated by Malcolm S. Walker.
       p. cm. -- (Simple science projects)
    Rev. ed. of: Colour and light. 1990.
    Includes bibliographical references and index.
    Summary: Explores color and light through projects involving kaleidoscopes, periscopes, shadow boxes, and other devices.
    ISBN 0-8368-0766-9
    1. Color--Experiments--Juvenile literature. 2. Lights--Experiments--Juvenile literature. [1. Color--Experiments. 2. Light--Experiments. 3. Experiments.] I. Walker, Malcolm S., ill. II. Williams, John. Colour and light. III. Title. IV. Series: Williams, John. Simple science projects.
QC495.5.W56 1992
535'.078--dc20
                                               91-50544

North American edition first published in MDCCCCLXXXXII by

Gareth Stevens Publishing
1555 North RiverCenter Drive, Suite 201
Milwaukee, Wisconsin 53212, USA

U.S. edition © MDCCCCLXXXXII by Gareth Stevens, Inc. First published as *Starting Technology — Colour and Light* in the United Kingdom, © MDCCCCLXXXXI by Wayland (Publishers) Limited. Additional end matter © MDCCCCLXXXXII by Gareth Stevens, Inc.

Editor (U.K.): Anna Girling
Editor (U.S.): Eileen Foran, Patricia Lantier-Sampon
Editorial assistant (U.S.): John D. Rateliff
Designer: Kudos Design Services
Cover design: Sharone Burris

Printed in the United States of America

2 3 4 5 6 7 8 9 97 96 95 94

CONTENTS

Words printed in **boldface** type appear in the glossary on pages 30-31.

Imagine living in a colorless world. There would be no green grass, no blue sky, and no bright clothes. It would be a very dull-looking world!

Most of our natural light comes from sunshine. Sunlight is made up of the seven colors of the **rainbow**: red, orange, yellow, green, blue, **indigo**, and violet. The three main colors are red, green, and blue. All the others are mixtures of these three colors.

Try to pick out the seven colors in this rainbow.

Experimenting with light

You will need:

*A **prism***
A bowl of water
Cooking oil
Paper and pencils

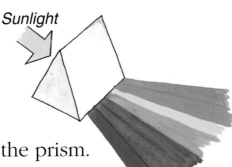

Sunlight

1. Look through the prism. Hold it close to your eyes. Can you see all sorts of colors shining through?

2. Pour a little oil on top of the water. Look for some of the same colors that you saw through the prism.

Sunlight

3. Collect as many different materials as you can. Try paper, wood, glass, and plastic. Hold each of them up to the light. Can you see through these materials? Can you see any shadows through them? Make a chart like this:

NAME OF MATERIAL	CAN SEE THROUGH	CAN SEE SHADOWS THROUGH	CANNOT SEE THROUGH
Paper			
Wood			
Glass			

Things that you can see through, like glass windows, are called **transparent**.

Further work

Red, green, and blue are the **primary colors** of sunlight. Take a sheet of **cellophane** in each of these colors. Hold them up to the light. Put one on top of another. What colors do you see?

Collect as many colored transparent candy and food wrappers as you can. Make a pattern or picture with them by sticking them onto a sheet of tracing paper. Tape your picture to a window.

5

MIXING COLORS

As we have seen in the experiment on page 5, the primary colors of sunlight are red, green, and blue. Red and green together make yellow. Red, green, and blue together make white.

The primary colors of painting are different from the colors of sunlight. They are red, yellow, and blue. Mixed together, they make dark brown.

These artists are using different mixtures of colors for their paintings.

Paints and dyes

You will need:

Paper
Paintbrushes
Paints (red, yellow, and blue)
Food **dyes** (red, yellow, blue,
  and green)
A transparent bowl of water

1. Draw pictures with any two primary colors. What other colors do these paints make when they are mixed together?

2. Now paint a picture using all three primary colors.

3. Put one or two drops of one of your food dyes into the bowl of water. Wait to see what happens when the dye mixes with the water. **Do not shake the bowl.** Now try this with the other colors.

Making a color box

You will need:

A shoe box
Cardboard
Felt-tip pens
Scissors
Glue
Colored sheets of cellophane
Tape

1. Draw a picture on one end of the box, on the inside.

2. Draw pictures on cardboard. Cut them out and glue them standing upright in the box.

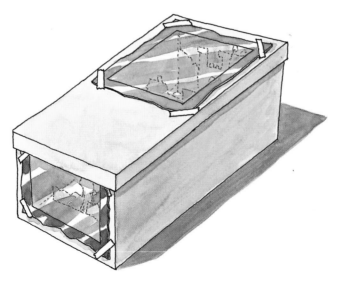

3. Cut a square hole in the lid of the box. Cut another hole at the front end of the box.

4. Tape colored cellophane over both of the holes. Now what color is your picture?

Making a pair of eyeglasses

You will need:

Cardboard
Scissors
Glue
Colored sheets of cellophane

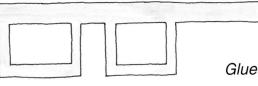

Glue

1. Cut out a frame for your eyeglasses from the cardboard, making sure it fits your face.

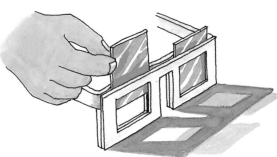

2. Cut out another piece of cardboard, exactly the same as the front part of the frame.

3. Glue this to the eyeglasses, but leave the top open.

4. Cut out pieces of cellophane and slide them into the top of the glasses. Try different colors.

Look at the colors in this glass window. Light shines through the glass to enhance the colored pattern.

Making colored spinners

You will need:

Cardboard
Felt-tip pens or crayons
A ruler
A sharpened pencil
Scissors

1. Draw a circle about 5 inches (12 cm) in **diameter** on the cardboard and cut it out.

2. Draw some lines through the middle of the circle so that it has eight equal parts. Color four sections yellow and four sections blue.

3. Make a tiny hole in the middle of the circle. Push a sharpened pencil through the hole so that you can spin the circle.

4. Spin the circle on the floor or a table top. When the circle spins fast, do you still see two colors? What color do you see as they blend together?

Further work

Cut out more circles and draw some different patterns on them. Use different colors. Do they all look alike when they are spinning?

This colored top is like the colored spinners you can make. Its colors blur when it spins.

Many animals use color to protect themselves or hide from enemies. This is called **camouflage**. Some animals are the same colors as the things around them. Others may be spotted or striped. Spots and stripes make an animal's shape difficult to see from a distance.

Can you see the little tree frog? It is the same color as the leaf it is sitting on.

Making camouflaged animals

You will need:
Cardboard
Felt-tip pens
Glue
Scissors
Thumbtacks

1. On cardboard, draw some pictures of different types of scenery. Draw a forest, a jungle, an underwater scene, and any other scenes you can think of. Do not draw any animals in your pictures.

2. Now draw some animals that you think would live in the type of scenery you have painted. Color them carefully to match your scenery pictures. Cut them out and glue a small strip of cardboard to them so that you can hold them up.

3. Tack your scenery pictures to the wall and hold the animals in front of each one. Ask a friend to stand away from the pictures and tell you which animals are hard to see. Those animals that are difficult to see are well camouflaged.

TIE-DYE

Tying and dyeing

You will need:

White cotton cloth
String
Rubber bands
Marbles
Cold-water dyes
Scissors

1. Cut out some pieces of cloth, each about the size of a large handkerchief.

2. Fold each piece in a different way and tie string or rubber bands tightly around them. You might tie them into a bundle, fold them into an accordian shape, knot them, twist them, or tie them over a marble.

Tied over a marble

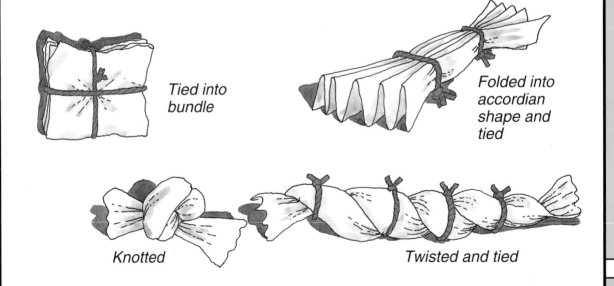

Tied into bundle

Folded into accordian shape and tied

Knotted

Twisted and tied

3. Soak the cloths in water and then put them into the dye solution (follow the instructions on the dye packet). When using dyes, it is a good idea to wear an apron and plastic gloves to protect your clothes and skin.

4. Rinse the cloths again. Now untie them and leave them on a flat surface to dry.

5. When they are dry, they should be ironed to make the dye stay in the cloth.

Further work

Different folds and ties make different patterns. On a large piece of cloth, draw a pattern that you would like to make. Use the patterns you have already made as guides. Tie your cloth to make the pattern and then dye it as before.

MIRRORS

Collect a small group of shiny things, such as metal spoons, glass objects, beads, or aluminum foil. Can you see yourself in any of them?

Look at yourself in a large, shiny spoon. Turn the spoon around. Do you look the same from both sides? A shiny spoon is like a curved mirror.

This is a pattern made by a kaleidoscope.

Making a kaleidoscope

You will need:

*Three small plastic mirrors,
  all the same size*
Cardboard
Tape
Tracing paper
Scissors
Sequins or small beads
Glue

1. Cut out three pieces of cardboard that are a little larger than the mirrors. Glue them to the backs of the mirrors.

2. Tape the pieces of cardboard together at the edges so that they make a triangular-shaped tube with the mirrors facing the inside.

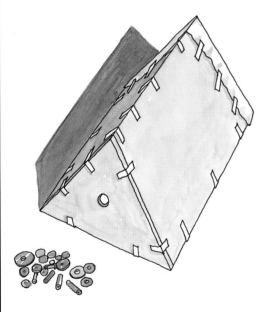

3. At one end, attach a triangle of cardboard that has a small peephole in the middle. At the other end, attach a piece of tracing paper. Put the sequins into the kaleidoscope through the hole.

4. Look through the peephole to see what patterns the sequins make on the three mirrors.

5. Now decorate the outside of your kaleidoscope. Paint some colored patterns on it.

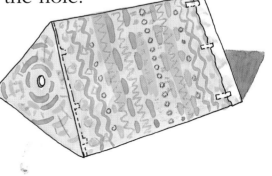

17

PERISCOPES

Hold two mirrors in front of you, one above the other. Tilt them so that when you look in the lower mirror you can see what is **reflected** by the upper mirror. A periscope in a **submarine** uses mirrors like this to see what is above the water.

It is often helpful to be able to see around corners. This mirror is positioned to help drivers see if a car is coming around a curve in the road.

Making a periscope

You will need:

Two mirrors, both the same size
Thick cardboard
Glue
Scissors

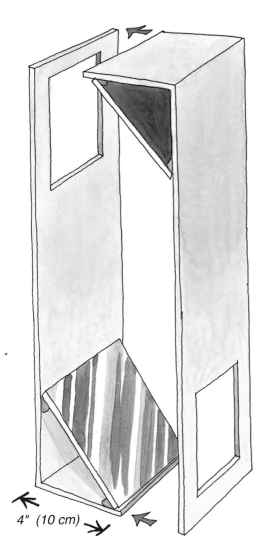

1. Cut two pieces of cardboard about 28 inches (70 cm) long and the same width as your mirrors. Fold each piece about 4 inches (10 cm) from the end.

2. Glue the mirrors across the folds of the cardboard, as shown. They should both be attached at exactly the same slant.

3. Cut out a square hole at the opposite ends of each piece of the cardboard.

4. Glue the two pieces together so that the mirrors are at either end of your periscope.

4" (10 cm)

5. Cut two more pieces of cardboard for the sides of your periscope and glue them in place.

6. Hold the periscope upright and look through the bottom hole. What do you see?

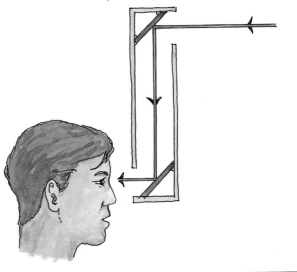

19

SHADOWS

Go outside on a sunny day. Look at your shadow. Is it a funny shape? Is it taller than you or shorter than you? Can you jump on your own shadow?

These shadows are very long. What time of the day do you think it is?

Making a shadow box theater

You will need:

A large shoe box
Cardboard
Tracing paper
Tape
Scissors
A flashlight

1. Cut a large square hole in one end of the box. Tape a piece of tracing paper over this end. This is your screen.

2. Cut a smaller round hole at the other end. Cut narrow slits across the bottom of the box.

3. Now draw some people and objects on cardboard and cut them out. Slide them through the slits into the box.

4. Shine a flashlight through the hole at the end of the box. Look for shadows on the screen at the other end. Do the shadows change at all when you move the flashlight farther away from the box?

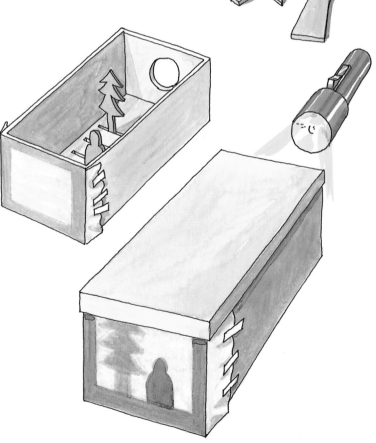

Have you ever seen a slide show at school or at a museum? A machine called a **projector** is used to show pictures on a wall or screen.

Look how much bigger the people in this picture are when they are seen through a magnifying glass.

Making a simple projector

You will need:

Cardboard	Tape
Felt-tip pens	A magnifying glass
A sheet of cellophane	A flashlight

1. Cut out a square frame from the cardboard.

2. Cut out a square of cellophane and draw a picture on it. Tape it to your frame.

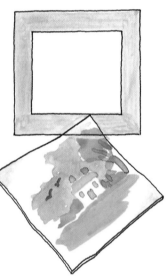

3. Hold the picture and the magnifying glass in front of a white wall.

4. Ask a friend to shine a flashlight so that the light goes through the picture, then through the magnifying glass, and onto the wall.

5. Move the picture and glass nearer and then farther away from the wall. Does the picture change? In what way?

A **microscope** uses **lenses** to make very small things look bigger. A **telescope** uses lenses to make things that are far away look closer.

Making a simple microscope

You will need:

A strip of thick cardboard about
  8 inches (20 cm) long and
  2 inches (5 cm) wide
A newspaper
A sewing needle
Water

1. Fold the cardboard ends as shown above.

2. Use the needle to make a hole in the middle of the cardboard.

3. Place your "microscope" on a page of the newspaper. Put your eye close to the hole and look for a letter on the page.

4. Put a drop of water on the cardboard, over the hole. Look again through the hole. Carefully move the folded ends in and out. Does this change the way the letter looks?

Making telescopes

You will need:

Magnifying lenses

A flat strip of wood about
  12 inches (30 cm) long

Modeling clay

Two cardboard tubes, one
  slightly larger than the other

Tape

1. Lenses come in many different shapes. The ones you need are called **convex** lenses. Both sides are curved outward. You will need a thick one and a thin one.

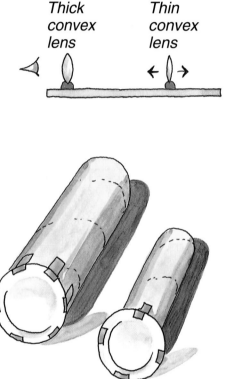

Thick convex lens

Thin convex lens

2. Use modeling clay to attach the thick lens to one end of the wood.

3. Slide the thin lens up and down the wood while looking through the thick lens. When you can look through both lenses and clearly see the wall on the other side of the room, secure the thin lens in position with modeling clay.

4. Move your telescope away from the wall. Does this make any difference to what you can see?

5. Now take the lenses off of the wood. Tape the thin lens to one end of the wider tube and the thick lens to one end of the narrow tube. Push the open end of the smaller tube into the wider tube.

6. Look through the thick lens. Move one tube inside the other until you get a clear picture.

LIGHT AND MOTION

Making a movie book

You will need:

Thick paper
Scissors
Felt-tip pens
Glue
A stapler

1. Cut out several pieces of thick paper about 5 inches (12 cm) long and about 2 1/2 inches (6 cm) wide.

2. On each piece of paper, draw a picture of a stick person running. Each picture should show a different stage of movement.

3. Glue and staple the papers together to make a book.

4. When you flip through the book, the stick person seems to be moving.

These are strips of film used in a movie. They move through a projector so fast that they create a "moving" picture.

A fish in a bowl

You will need:

Paper   A small wooden rod
Scissors   Glue
Felt-tip pens

1. Cut out a piece of stiff paper about 4 inches (10 cm) square. On one side draw a fish and on the other side draw a fishbowl.

2. Glue the paper to the end of the wooden rod, as shown.

3. Spin the rod. As the paper spins, the fish will seem to be in its bowl.

Mirror tricks

You will need:

Paper
Pens
A mirror

1. Write some large letters on a piece of paper.

2. Put the edge of the mirror next to the paper, so that it reflects the letters. Do some of the letters look different in the mirror? Do some look the same?

3. Put the edge of the mirror right through the middle of the letters. Look at the patterns the letters make in the mirror.

What You'll Need

More Books About Color and Light

All About Colors. Ruth Thomson (Gareth Stevens)
The Color Kittens. Margaret Wise Brown (Western Publishing)
Hailstones & Halibut Bones: Adventures in Color. Mary O'Neill (Zephyr)
Light. Rocco V. Feravolo (Garrard)
Light! Color! Action! Tom Johnston (Gareth Stevens)
Light and Color. L. W. Anderson (Raintree)
Light and Lasers. Kathryn Whyman (Franklin Watts)
Light Fantastic. Philip Watson (Lothrop, Lee & Shepard)
The Magic of Color. Hilda Seymour (Lothrop, Lee & Shepard)
Mirrors. Julie Fitzpatrick (Silver Burdett)
Of Colors and Things. Tana Hoban (Greenwillow)

More Books With Projects

Bouncing and Bending Light. Barbara Taylor (Franklin Watts)
I Can Make a Rainbow. Marjorie Frank (Incentive)
Light. Eiji Orii and Masako Orii (Gareth Stevens)
Light and Color. Jerry DeBruin (Good Apple)
Me & My Shadow. Joy Joyce (Joy-Co Press)
My Big FunThinker Book of Light. Laura Cohen (Educational Insights)
Paper Kaleidoscopes. Kay Leonard (Pelona Press)
Shadow Magic. Seymour Simon (Lothrop, Lee & Shepard)

Places to Write for Science Supply Catalogs

Edmund Scientific
101 East Gloucester Pike
Barrington, New Jersey 08007

The Nature of Things
275 West Wisconsin Avenue
Milwaukee, Wisconsin 53203

Nasco Science
901 Janesville Road
Fort Atkinson, Wisconsin 53538

Adventures in Science
Educational Insights
19560 Rancho Way
Dominguez Hills, California 90220

Suitcase Science
Small World Toys
P. O. Box 5291
Beverly Hills, California 90209

GLOSSARY

camouflage
The way animals hide themselves by looking like the things around them.

cellophane
A thin sheet of clear plastic.

convex
Curved outward.

diameter
The length of a straight line going through the center of a circle from one side to the other.

dyes
Materials used to change the color of something.

indigo
A dark blue-purple color.

lens
A clear plastic material, such as glass or plastic, that is curved to bend the rays of light passing through it.

microscope
A device for making small things look large.

primary colors
The three main colors of light or painting. All other colors are made by mixing primary colors together.

prism
A clear, triangular-shaped piece of glass. Prisms split the light passing through them into the seven colors of the rainbow.

projector
A machine that projects an image onto a screen.

rainbow
An arc of color that is seen in the sky opposite the Sun. It is caused by the Sun's rays shining through raindrops.

reflect
To bounce light off of a shiny surface, such as a mirror.

submarine
A ship that can operate both underwater and on the surface.

telescope
A device for making faraway things look closer.

transparent
Clear; able to be seen through.

Picture acknowledgements
The publishers would like to thank the following for allowing their photographs to be reproduced in this book: Chapel Studios, pp. 9, 11, 26; Eye Ubiquitous, pp. 16, 18, 22; Oxford Scientific Films, p. 12; Science Photo Library, p. 4; Tony Stone Worldwide, p. 6; Timothy Woodcock, p. 20. Cover photography by Zul Mukhida.

INDEX